STEAM
ENGINES
EXPLAINED

ST

COUNTRYSIDE BOOKS
NEWBURY BERKSHIRE

First published 2009
© Stan Yorke 2009

COUNTRYSIDE BOOKS
3 Catherine Road
Newbury, Berkshire

To view our complete range of books,
please visit us at
www.countrysidebooks.co.uk

ISBN 978 1 84674 149 4

Photographs by the author
Illustrations by Trevor Yorke

Designed by Peter Davies, Nautilus Design
Produced through MRM Associates Ltd., Reading
Typeset by CJWT Solutions, St Helens
Printed by Information Press, Oxford

CONTENTS

Introduction

Today we have become so used to a regular stream of new products and developments that it is very easy to forget that our progress over the centuries has been marked by a small number of inventions of enormous importance. These have often arrived gradually without that Eureka! moment for historians to write about and record. The discovery of iron was one; the invention, for want of a better word, of steel (which predates the Roman Empire and which over time led to the steel we all rely on today) would certainly be another. So would printing, held by many as the greatest single invention made by man. The steam engine possibly also deserves to be on such a list for without it the Industrial Revolution would have petered out

Pre-steam factory power, locked to a good stream or river and dependent on the weather, but relatively cheap.

Two examples of the basic workshop engine (see Chapter 3).

Both can be regularly seen working in the Markham Grange Steam Museum, near Doncaster.

with just the canals and some very impressive water wheels.

Whilst to most of us today the term 'steam engine' probably means a railway locomotive, in fact throughout the 19th century it featured in almost every aspect of life. It enabled deep mines to produce the extraordinary quantities of coal that kept industry working and our homes warm. It drove the factories that made Britain the leading industrial nation of the century and by the 1880s it powered ships, canal boats, cars, buses and trams as well. All these activities have long passed over to the internal combustion engine or to electricity. Here is one of life's little surprises, for whilst the steam engine drove the first electricity generators – it still does! Roughly half of the world's electricity is still produced courtesy of the steam engine, including almost all of our supplies here in Britain.

In this book I have used a fairly wide definition of the term 'steam engine'. Basically, if a machine takes steam as its input and produces mechanical movement as its output then it is a steam engine. I want to follow the story of these machines from their shaky start, through the frantic 19th century to the birth of mechanical transport and on to today's turbines.

Stan Yorke

CHAPTER 1

How It All Started

T he seeds were sown a long way back in time. Hero of Alexandria had understood that gases expand and contract when heated and cooled. In 1606 the pressure of steam lifting water had been demonstrated, as had the force of a vacuum, though the reason for this wasn't understood. Nearly 40 years were to pass before it was realized that the atmosphere had weight and it was this that produced the power, not the vacuum itself. Further people experimented, slowly adding to the understanding of gases, until in 1690

FIG 1.1: *In 1698 the Cornish engineer Savery patented a machine for 'Raising of Water by the Impellant Force of Fire' aimed at pumping water out of mine workings.*

Denis Papin used condensing steam to draw a piston into a cylinder. Though he only made an experimental model with a piston just 2½ inches in diameter he had in fact demonstrated the first atmospheric engine.

I must mention the work of Thomas Savery for, though his work led to very little, he was the first to see a real application for steam. His idea was to position his machine halfway down a mine shaft and, using condensing steam, to raise water up to the machine then, using steam pressure, to push the water up to the surface. First, steam from the boiler was admitted to the cylinder. Once full, valves were closed and the cylinder was douched in cold water. This made the steam condense, producing a vacuum which caused the water below to rise and fill the cylinder. Valves were now opened and steam from the boiler admitted, which forced the water out of the cylinder and up the pipe towards the surface. Again the valves were closed, the empty but steam-filled cylinder was cooled and the cycle repeated. Savery proposed two cylinders which alternated – one being cooled whilst steam was warming the other. As far as I know it never entered service in mines and, though technically feasible, the ironwork of the day simple couldn't meet the machine's needs.

Another engineer in Cornwall,

Thomas Newcomen, worked on similar ideas, inspired by an attempt to repair a Savery engine when the cylinder collapsed under the partial vacuum inside it. Amazed at the apparently vast power of atmospheric pressure he experimented for nearly 15 years before he was able to erect his first atmospheric engine at a coal mine near Dudley Castle in 1712.

These machines were very inefficient but they had several fundamental features which ensured their success. Firstly they were mechanically simple: they used technology that was readily

FIG 1.2: *A replica of Newcomen's first engine at the Black Country Living Museum, Dudley – close to where the first engine was erected.*

available, and they could be made and erected by the engineers of the day. Most of all they worked and were very reliable, two qualities that were still rare in the early 18th century. If a date needs to be given for the moment when man freed himself from depending on animals, water and wind for power it was 1712.

Two well-known names now appear: John Smeaton and James Watt, who further developed Newcomen's engine between them, achieving much greater efficiency and power output. Smeaton achieved an increase in power by careful design changes and improvements in the accuracy and size of cylinders. Watt, who is named in myth as the 'Inventor of the Steam Engine', was in fact a very careful craftsman who worked in Glasgow University as an instrument maker. In 1763 he was asked to repair a faulty working model of a Newcomen engine, and during this work he slowly realized why it was so inefficient. Six years later he patented his separate condenser idea and four years after that entered into a partnership with the industrialist Matthew Boulton. As Boulton & Watt they produced some of the finest engines of the time, consuming less than a third of the coal needed by the original Newcomen engines for the same output.

It was at this same time, 1774, that John Wilkinson had developed a boring machine at his works in Bersham near Wrexham, originally designed for boring cannon barrels and still turned by a water wheel. This enabled cast-iron cylinders to be used rather than the

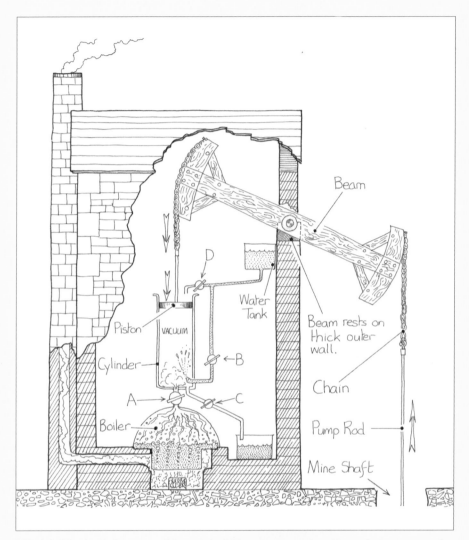

Labels on diagram: Beam; Water Tank; Piston; VACUUM; Cylinder; A; B; C; D; Boiler; Beam rests on thick outer wall.; Chain; Pump Rod; Mine Shaft

FIG 1.3: *The basic features of the original Newcomen engine. First admit steam to the cylinder via valve A. Next close A and condense the steam by opening B to produce a spray of cold water into the cylinder. The natural air pressure forces the piston down producing the power stroke, raising the outside end of the beam and the pump rod going down the mine shaft. Valve B is now closed and C is opened to drain the condensed steam and air. The weight of the pump rods now pulls the outside end of the beam back down thus raising the piston. Valve D allows water to be run on top of the piston to aid in maintaining a good seal against the surface of the cylinder walls.*

FIG 1.4: *The top of an early cast-iron cylinder showing the piston, which would be kept wet to help the seal.*

FIG 1.5: *The much reinforced wooden beam of Watt's Smethwick pump engine. (The Think Tank)*

earlier and expensive brass cylinders used by Newcomen. Early cast iron was too rough to use without being machined. This coupling of Watt's developments to improved and machined cast iron took the steam engine from lumbering pumping engines to becoming a universal tool. Sizes and power soon grew and it became common for massive machines to have cylinders of six feet in diameter, with equally amazing strokes.

One last development was the idea of re-using the spent steam from one cylinder by allowing it to expand further in a larger 'low pressure' cylinder, with both cylinders driving the same beam or shaft. This was called 'compound working'. Early engines used relatively low steam pressures at all stages, so the idea produced little improvement in efficiency at first and, until higher pressure boilers arrived at the start of the 19th century, it had to wait to find acclaim.

Boulton was aware that most industrial processes had grown up using the rotating power produced by the water wheel or the windmill and pressed Watt to apply himself to converting the rocking motion of his engines to produce a rotating output. Though Watt had several patents on his engines many other engineers were also working on steam power. One of his

FIG 1.6: *The cylinder of the Smethwick engine with its seemingly complicated valve mechanism.*

ex-pupils, James Pickard, was ahead of Watt and patented the common crank to produce rotation. Watt, rather than challenge the patent, evolved the sun and planet gear instead, although near to the end of Pickard's patent (1794) Boulton & Watt began producing engines using the simple crank.

As we approach the end of the 18th century we find the simple and rugged Newcomen engines still the favourite for pumping water from mines but the rotative engine being produced by many companies was setting industry alight with excitement. Factories were now free from the moods of the weather and the need to be near a stream or river.

CHAPTER 2

How A Steam Engine Works

In this chapter I am going to get a little more technical and explain the way the early engines worked, and then follow their development through to the 20th century. All these engines are classed as heat engines, in that the original source of their energy is derived from heat. The heat produced by burning coal or wood is used to generate steam which can be used in two completely different ways.

Atmospheric engines

One of the things that makes steam engines attractive is that one can see most of what's going on! The one aspect a drawing cannot show easily is the sequence of events that make it work. Newcomen put together this sequence and turned a series of known features into a working machine – this sounds obvious today but it was an enormous step in 1712. Atmospheric engines use the fact that steam occupies a much greater space than the water from which it comes (around 1500 times the water volume). When steam is condensed by cooling it returns to liquid form and occupies its original volume. If it has been contained in a sealed cylinder then this cooling produces a partial vacuum.

The sequence is as follows: let the weight of the pump rods going down the mine shaft pull on the beam and thus raise the piston up to the top of the cylinder. Remember Newcomen was only concerned with pumping water out of mines. Next fill the space below the piston with steam, shut off the steam and spray cold water into the cylinder to cool the steam down. This condenses the steam, creating a partial vacuum beneath the piston and the natural atmospheric pressure now forces the piston downwards into the space once occupied by the steam,

FIG 2.1: *The first Haystack boilers had a lead top but soon this was replaced by riveted iron plates. (Blists Hill Museum, Ironbridge)*

producing the power stroke. We must now get the condensed water out of the bottom of the cylinder and wait for the weight of the pump rods to drag the piston back to the top, drawing steam from the boiler into the cylinder as it rises – cycle complete. In the earliest machines the steam valve and the cooling water valve were controlled manually by the driver. Rates of up to 12 strokes a minute were achieved, hour after hour. Very soon it was realized that these valves are required to operate at fixed points in the cycle and the manual valves were replaced with valves operated from the beam, producing the first free-running engine.

There are, however, a few points to note. The upward stroke is controlled by the weight of the pump rods – given no restraint the beam will simply accelerate until it hits the end stops with an almighty bang. The downward, or power, stroke depends on the steam condensing and this produces the opposite movement – fast at first but then slowing once most of the steam has condensed. Indeed, how far the piston descends depends on the amount of steam in the cylinder and, possibly, the stroke might not even reach the bottom. These differences produce a slightly jerky and uneven motion. The running, however, depends completely on those rarely mentioned items – the valves, vital to all reciprocating engines.

It was whilst pondering this sequence of events that Watt realized that the cylinder was being heated when the steam entered but was then cooled down by the condensing phase. In fact as the steam entered the cool cylinder condensing started straight away on the cylinder's surfaces, in effect reducing the quantity of steam left to do the real work. This heating/cooling wasted much of the energy in the steam and Watt's solution was to do the condensing in a separate vessel, leaving the working cylinder to remain hot all the time. Later, Watt devised the means to pass steam around the outside of the cylinder, thus keeping it almost as hot as the steam itself.

Watt continued to make advances. The next was to seal the top of the cylinder and pass steam, not just below the piston to create the condensing power stroke, but also above the piston to help the downward motion. When the piston was drawn upwards, a

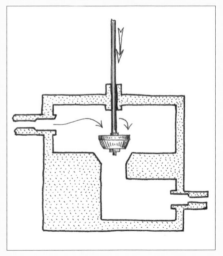

FIG 2.2: *Basic bath plug valve which needs a good pull to lift it up against the pressure of the steam.*

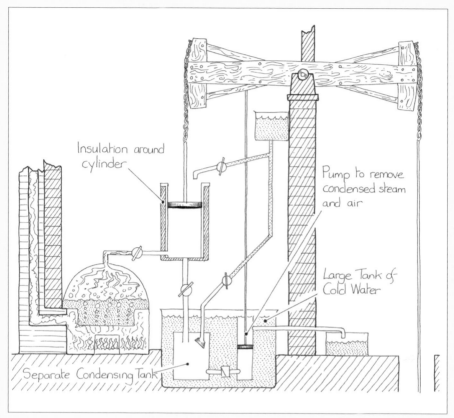

FIG 2.3: *Watt's first major improvement, the separate condenser. Though on this drawing I have shown the valves as simple taps, by this time they would have been worked by linkages from the beam.*

so-called equalizing valve opened which allowed the steam above the piston to flow to below the piston ready for the next power stroke. The next step followed from passing steam above the piston to gain a little more power. Why not have a second condensing phase using the steam above the piston? This would now provide a power stroke on both the downward and upward strokes. It is called 'double working' and produces almost twice the power from the one cylinder. This meant of course that the piston was now pushing the beam upwards as well as drawing it down. In order to use both the downward stroke and the upward push created by double working a different system to the arc and chain had to be devised – the chain

FIG 2.4: *Watt's double acting engine. Steam is admitted via valve A to add a little downward push, but also to fill the cylinder above the piston whilst valve D is open and is condensing the steam below the piston to provide the main downward power stroke. At the bottom of the stroke the tables are turned and valve C admits steam below the piston whilst valve B opens to cause the condensing upward power stroke. Under this arrangement the top of the cylinder is now sealed and a gland allows the piston rod to move up and down whilst retaining the steam.*

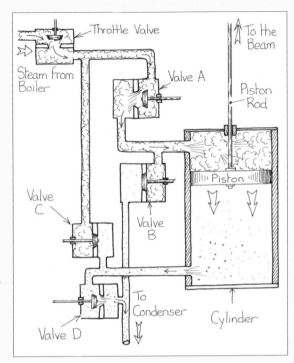

could pull but it couldn't push. Watt produced what he always felt was his best idea – the parallel motion linkage which enables the piston rod to move in a straight line whilst pushing and pulling the beam end, which of course has to follow an arc.

These machines were not intended to operate in mine pumping where the pull-only stroke of the earlier engines is all that is needed. These were to be used to produce rotation. These rotating machines now challenged the waterwheel, being able to deliver power wherever it was needed. Indeed, some water wheels and windmills had a steam engine to take over

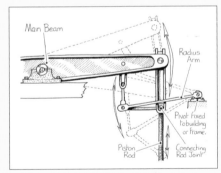

FIG 2.5: *Watt's parallel linkage, which kept the top of the piston rod moving in a straight line despite the arc traced by the end of the beam. Being a solid linkage it could push the beam up as well as pull it down.*

FIG 2.6: *Watt's parallel motion in action. This beam engine produces rotation and used to wind trucks up the Middleton Incline in Derbyshire.*

when there was insufficient water or wind.

Pressure Engines

The second way to use steam is to employ the steam directly to push a piston. The cylinder now acts as a container to keep the steam confined while the piston moves. The important point is that the steam pressure can be much higher than the 12 or so pounds per square inch of the atmospheric engine, allowing a smaller engine to produce the same power as the lumbering giant beam engines. The change from atmospheric working to pressure working, however, is confused by the use of medium steam pressures (up to 50 lb/in^2) and atmospheric

working within the same engine. The famous Cornish engine developed by Richard Trevithick is an example of this dual working.

The pressure engine is probably easier to understand as it simply uses the steam to push a piston along a sealed cylinder. All that is required is to let the steam in and then to let the used steam out again at the right moment – using our friend the valve again.

There is one trick that enables the efficiency to be improved: that is to admit the steam for a short time and then allow the steam to expand on its own, still pushing the piston. This doesn't produce as much power as letting the full steam pressure complete the entire stroke but it uses far less steam. This is nicely demonstrated if you watch a steam locomotive. When starting off, the exhaust roars up the chimney with terrific force. This is because the steam is pushing the piston at full pressure over nearly the whole stroke to achieve maximum power. At the end of the stroke the steam is still at full pressure and when the exhaust valve opens, high-pressure steam escapes with gusto. Once under way the steam is admitted to the cylinder for only part of the stroke and, having expanded, the final pressure is less which in turn produces less of a blast when the exhaust valve is opened. This produces the steady soft stream of smoke and steam from the locomotive's chimney once under way.

Watt was always cautious about steam pressure, having started his career when boilers and ironwork were weak. By 1790 several engineers were working on higher pressure engines, including Trevithick who produced a steam-engined road vehicle in 1802. The roads of the day just couldn't carry the weight so he turned to the tramways where, after the strength of the rails was improved, his

FIG 2.7: *A GWR loco getting under way on the West Somerset Railway with only a small cut-off applied.*

FIG 2.8: *A replica of Trevithick's 1801 road vehicle, made to celebrate his bicentenary, having its own road test, this time on tarmac. (The Trevithick Society)*

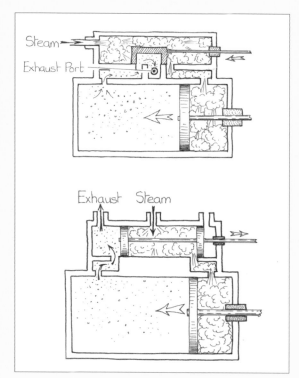

Steam

Exhaust Port

Exhaust   Steam

FIG 2.9: *The slide valve and below the later piston valve. Both work in a similar manner: by moving the valve rod it is possible to introduce steam at one side of the piston while it is leaving the other, or the other way around.*

locomotives started the railway revolution.

Because it is relatively simple to achieve, most steam engines from the early 19th century onwards were double working, and condensing steam for atmospheric working disappeared. There is of course always an exception and this was Trevithick's Cornish engine, which used a pressure stroke followed by a condensing steam atmospheric stroke and which continued to be produced up to the 1850s.

Both the slide valve and the piston valve produce double working, that is both the forward and backward strokes generate power.

The majority of engines built during the 19th century produced rotating motion by using a simple crank to convert the to and fro motion of the piston into rotation. There is one problem with the crank and that is that the joint between the piston rod and the crank rod experiences an alternating sideways thrust which has to be contained to prevent the piston rod and the piston from being moved out of line with the cylinder. This is achieved by having a guide mechanism which absorbs these sideways pressures and,

FIG 2.10: *The crosshead guides can be clearly seen on this view of GWR locomotive No. 5199 taken on the Severn Valley Railway. The guides hold the joint between the piston and the connecting rod (the crosshead) and keep it moving in a straight line.*

now usually mounted close to the cylinder in a valve chest and operated by rods actuated from the crank shaft. Difficulties arose for engines that need to vary the length of time that steam is admitted to the cylinder but to keep the exhaust phase constant. Valve mechanism design was always a compromise between keeping the mechanism simple, and easy to lubricate and maintain, and getting the timing perfect for maximum efficiency.

Over the years the optimum working evolved and I will attempt to describe the full cycle to show just how complex the job of the valves is. If we start with the piston at one end of the stroke then the job is to let steam in behind the

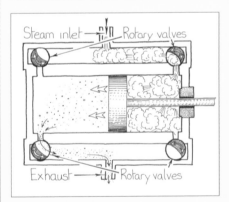

FIG 2.11: *The Corless valve, which was very common in the USA, uses four rotating valves which are swung from open to closed by cranks on the outside of the cylinder assembly. The big advantage is that the inlet operation is independent from the exhaust so the ideal timing for cut-off operation can be set easily without altering the exhaust timing.*

like Watt's parallel motion linkage, keeps the piston rod moving in a straight line. Constructed in various forms they all do the same basic job.

Valves

We have already met the basic 'bath plug' valve where the requirement was to pass or block the flow of large volumes of low-pressure steam. As the pressures increased smaller volumes were involved and the speed of the engines also increased which led to a series of bewildering valve designs. To keep the steam flowing quickly into and out of the cylinder the valves were

Inlet
Valves

Exhaust
Valves

FIG 2.12: *The Corless valves on a large mill engine. The bottom two are operated by a straightforward linkage but the top two, the steam inlet valves, are more complex to allow for cut-off working. This superb machine (named 'Agnes') can be seen working in the Markham Grange Steam Museum.*

piston to push it along the cylinder. At the same time we need to let the used steam pass out from in front of the piston. When the piston reaches the far end of the stroke the action is simply reversed. To produce cut-off, that is to let steam in for only a part of the stroke, we need to be able to shut off the steam entering the cylinder and we need to be able to alter when this cut takes place. Experimental work soon highlighted another desirable feature. If we close the exhaust valve just before the piston reaches the end of the stroke, the steam left behind acts as a cushion to help the piston slow down and reverse direction. Lastly, if we admit the steam that is to drive the piston back just a moment before the piston reverses, the steam has time to fill the pipework and valve chambers, so that by the time the piston has reversed steam pressure is building up with no time lag.

Steam locomotives and many other steam engines used piston valves in which the exhaust valve and inlet valves were combined in a way similar to the slide valve. The valve piston or slide covered or revealed the steam ports as it moved to and fro. This enabled a single steam inlet port and a single exhaust pipe to be used, making the pipework, particularly the high-pressure pipes, simple. The critical timing is achieved by the physical position and size of the valve piston or slide and the timing of the valve movement.

Compound engines

In the drive to increase efficiency, engineers realized that, to get all the

FIG 2.13: *A 1863 London-built two-cylinder compound beam engine made to pump water. The 17½ inch high-pressure cylinder is nearest the camera and the 30 inch low-pressure cylinder is to the left. Working on 60 lb/in^2 it produced 60 hp and turned at a stately 18 rpm.*

energy from the steam, it needs to be allowed to expand until there is almost no pressure left. This implies a long stroke but in turn brings back our old problem of the cylinder cooling down as the steam expands and then heating up again when the fresh full-pressure steam is admitted for the next stroke. What was needed was to extend the steam's journey into two or more cylinders with the steam slowly losing its pressure in stages. Now the temperature drop in each cylinder is reduced, improving efficiency. Thus was born the compound engine, initially with one high-pressure cylinder and one low-pressure cylinder. The exhaust steam from the higher-pressure cylinder is passed into a storage cylinder from which the valve gear of the second cylinder takes its supply. This reservoir evens out the inevitable peaks and troughs of pressure between the two cylinders.

These two-cylinder compound engines soon grew to three stages and these machines became common for all high-power steam engines, particularly in ships where carrying enough coal for a long journey was always a problem and every last improvement in efficiency was vital. Four-stage machines were also made but the improvement in efficiency was too small to justify the costs and extra weight.

The use of steam engines on ocean-going ships also raised another problem – water supply. Sea water is too corrosive for use in boilers so ships had to carry water, as well as coal. Then someone revisited the idea of condensing the used steam, not to produce any power but simply to regain the water. This water is pure and ideal for the boilers and condensing became common in other applications

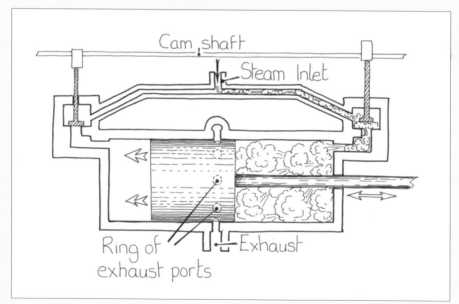

FIG 2.14: *The uniflow engine makes use of the piston to act as the exhaust valve thus needing only the inlet valves to be driven. This makes it very easy to apply variable cut-off.*

as well as ships. The Metropolitan Railway (London Underground) used condensing engines, partly to avoid the steam filling the tunnels, but also to reduce the amount of water that needed to be carried.

There is just one further reciprocating steam engine design to describe, which evolved partly to overcome the cooling effects within the cylinders. This is the uniflow engine, which avoids the constant reversing of the steam flow through the cylinder ports which, in a conventional engine, pass both the fresh steam in and the exhausted steam out. The uniflow engine was a relative latecomer to the scene and many of the engines built in the last 20 or 30 years of the steam era were of this type. In this engine the piston is very wide and acts as the exhaust valve, as well as providing the power output. The exhaust port has become a ring of ports around the centre of the cylinder, giving a large total area. Like nearly all the later engines these were usually fitted with condensers which not only recover the water from the exhausting steam but, just as Newcomen had done 200 years earlier, produce a partial vacuum which helps to draw the exhaust steam out of the cylinder quickly. There are two inlet valves operated by cams on a rotating shaft – very similar to the valves in a motor car. These engines were very efficient and were made in single- and double-acting and compound versions. They were also capable of running at high speeds and indeed were often used to generate electricity before the turbine appeared.

Turbines

Though many had played with using a jet of steam to turn a fan, it was not until the 1880s that C. A. Parsons developed the idea into a useful

FIG 2.15: *Little more than a novelty, the Aeolipile showed that a jet of steam produces a force. Described by Hero of Alexandria in the first century AD.*

FIG 2.16: *Early water turbine. High-pressure water from a higher reservoir entered on the right and spun the turbine. This unit was used to generate electricity in Caudwell Mill, Rowsley, Derbyshire.*

machine. Crude turbines that used water had been in use since 1000 BC, to grind flour. By the 12th century windmills, simple turbines, had evolved and today we have the modern version in wind farms generating electricity. Water turbines continued to develop during the 19th century and indeed worked into the mid-20th century generating electricity.

During the 100 years between 1785 and 1885 nearly 200 patents had been taken out on gas or steam turbines in England alone and some had actually started to get close to the final solution. The principle was to set the steam in motion, thus exchanging its pressure energy for kinetic or moving energy. By passing this flow through a turbine blade, rotation resulted. Parsons appreciated that the way to extract all the energy was to pass the ever-expanding steam through turbine after turbine, each operating at a slightly lower pressure but all mounted on the same shaft so all their individual contributions added together. To stop the steam flow from simply rotating, and to keep its approach to the blades optimum, a ring of static blades is placed between the rotating blades.

A turbine set generates reaction forces which cause great pressure on the end of the rotating shaft. Parsons built two opposite-facing turbines on a common shaft with the steam moving from the centre to the ends: thus the two machines spent their life in a massive tug of war, placing almost no thrust on the end bearings. Most turbine machines use this double set arrangement. To prevent problems with water vapour, turbines always use superheated steam, i.e. steam that has been reheated to achieve higher temperatures and 'dry' it. The initial drive for the development of these

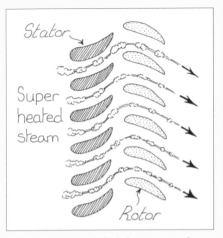

FIG 2.17: *A simplified diagram to show how the path of the steam is redirected by the static blades before hitting the next fan blade.*

machines had been to generate electricity and Parsons's first turbine, operating on 80 lbs/in^2, drove a 7 kW dynamo. To generate our normal 50 Hz mains electricity a speed of 3,000 rpm is ideal but turbines are more efficient running faster so many machines used gears to reduce the speed and gain torque. Being a purely rotating machine with no reciprocating mechanism they produce very little vibration. This is also part of the secret of their efficiency. In a reciprocating machine, much of the energy produced is used in the endless process of accelerating the piston then slowing it down, reversing the direction and accelerating it again.

Parsons also believed his turbines would be effective in driving ships but

FIG 2.18: *The turbine-blade assembly from an early Parsons' turbine used to drive a ship. Each of the twelve turbine blades runs between fixed static guide blades, each pair forming a turbine. Note that, in this example, the high-pressure steam enters at the ends and works towards the centre.*

was unable to interest the Admiralty. True to his determined nature he had his own demonstration boat built, the *Turbinia*. Sleek and with a beautiful underwater shape it was fitted with three turbines in a triple compound arrangement with each stage driving one of the three propellors. To complete the set a fourth turbine was fitted to the central propellor shaft to provide reverse. In a wonderful David and Goliath scene he turned up at the 1897 Spithead Review and raced between the assembled ships at an unheard of 34 knots! The point was made and the first turbine-driven commercial ship, the Clyde steamer *King Edward* was launched in 1901. Just ten years after his spectacular demonstration the 38,000 ton *Mauritania* achieved 26 knots driven by steam turbines.

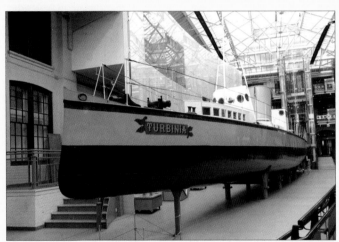

FIG 2.19: *Centre piece of the Newcastle Discovery Museum: the turbine-driven* Turbinia.

FIG 2.20: *The* Turbinia *on one of her many dramatic demonstration runs.*

CHAPTER 3

Stationary Engines

A stationary engine is simply one that is installed in a permanent building and is usually devoted to one specific use. Pumping water from coal and tin mines was the original reason that steam engines were developed and pumping remained one of the uses well into the 1950s. This long life is in part due to the basic requirement that a pumping engine must be able to run continuously year after year with a minimum of servicing. These engines thus tended to be over-engineered, simple, very reliable and indeed long-lived.

Beam engines were quickly applied to pumping water from rivers and wells for public water supplies, and by the 1850s to pumping sewage from town centres out to treatment works or just out to sea. Being utilitarian and often built using public money these great beam pumps were housed in splendid buildings and were decorated with full Victorian grandeur.

One rather unexpected use was made of beam engines: to pump air to drive the fires used in iron making. It was the use of forced air from waterwheel-driven bellows to enliven the fires that made the first important breakthrough in blast furnaces and, as iron making

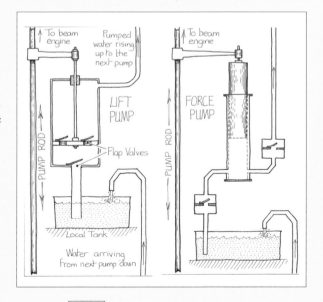

FIG 3.1: *The two basic pumps used for fluids. The lift pump (left) does its work on the upward stroke which was how the early beam engines were designed to operate. The force pump (right) does its work on the downward stroke and was commonly used in water and sewage pumping.*

FIG 3.2: *One of the grandest, Papplewick pumping station with two beautifully restored beam engines. Built by the James Watt Company in 1884 they pumped water from 200 feet below ground to supply Nottingham. Like most big engines there is a mezzanine floor to give access to the tops of the cylinders (a) and a full top floor (b) where the beams can be reached for maintenance. As was common on all these massive machines, the paintwork is delightful, the metal surfaces are all polished and everywhere is spotlessly clean.*

FIG 3.3: *The clever way that large bearings were made to allow for wear and to permit the bearing surfaces to be easily replaced. The bronze bearing (square with rounded corners) is split into two halves. These grip the round crank pin and are held in the upward-facing, U-shaped clip by the end of the connecting rod rising up to the beam. Two opposing wedges which are tightened by the bolts on the right join the clip to the end of the connecting rod.*

FIG 3.4: *The pumps used to move water were often force pumps housed in the basement of the pump house a few yards below the engine. As this did not involve the long pump links in mines, which pulled the beam down, a massive extra weight was added to the pump linkage and it was this weight that did the work of forcing the water upwards. The engine only raised the weight. This system had an advantage for water works, as the pressure applied to the water was now constant – it depended only on the weight and not on how well the engine was being driven. This monster is the weight from one of the old beam pumps at the Kew Bridge Steam Museum at Brentford.*

FIG 3.5: *One of the largest furnace blowing engines on display, this two-cylinder beam engine has a large flywheel to smooth out the motion. The power cylinders are nearest the camera and the two massive air-pumping cylinders are on the right. The valves for the double-action engine are in the house-shaped box by the top of the power cylinders. There are matching units at the bottom, just out of sight. (Blists Hill Museum, Ironbridge)*

expanded, bigger and bigger furnaces needed ever bigger air blowers.

Industry-driving machines

Once engines could provide rotating power the steam engine slowly replaced the waterwheel and windmill in industry. Led by the cotton and wool factories, where enormous engines powered an entire multi-floor factory, they came to be used in virtually every industry as the main source of power for over 100 years. These belt-driven looms were known for the danger caused by the small space between the machines and the unprotected belts. If the belt broke or became split, the time lost mending it was deducted from the machine operator's meagre wages. Therefore, it became common to make a rough mend using staples to hold a patch in place. After several such mends, however, the belt became a fast-moving death trap, the staples gripping anything that touched the belt, be it hair or clothes, and the victim would literally be swept up and into the machinery. The smaller engines capable

FIG 3.6: *Steam engines revolutionized getting men and materials in and out of mines. This restored winding engine is typical of that used in the hundreds of small mines throughout the UK.*

of 10 to 30 hp were easy to install and provided more power than most waterwheels. They were used to drive winding gear in mines, providing a quick and reliable means of lifting and lowering both men and the minerals. In factories and workshops it was standard practice to have the boiler house and the engine outside and to take the power to the various machines via a system of belts driven from pulley shafts that ran along just below the roof, all driven from the engine house.

The boilers are the rather poor relation to all this shining metal and paintwork, even more so as (at least until the 1880s) they invariably involved shovelling coal. The earliest boilers had the fire directly heating the bottom and lower sides of the boiler but soon furnace tube boilers appeared, in which the fire burnt at one end of the boiler and the smoke and fumes passed through large tubes which ran through the water to heat it. To make the most of the heat contained in the smoke it was normal to take the exhaust around the outside of the boiler before sending

FIG 3.7: *Probably the most dramatic steam engines of all – the mill engines. This relatively modern machine drove a 16-ft diameter rope drum which transferred its power to pulley shafts throughout the mill.*

FIG 3.8: *A sample of the 2¾-inch rope used with this engine. These drive ropes could last up to 20 years.*

FIG 3.9: *The pulley and belt system for driving machinery lasted well into the 1950s, even in really large workshops. Accidents, however, were still quite common and sometimes fatal. This vast machine shop in the Queen Street Mill, Burnley, is driven by a working mill engine called 'Peace'.*

FIG 3.10: *Each machine had a mechanism which allowed the belt to be moved sideways to run over a free-wheeling pulley – in effect, a neutral gear.*

FIG 3.11: *The Lancashire boiler as seen by the stoker. They were usually built into a brick housing around which the smoke circulated before going up the chimney. Tall chimneys were needed to generate a strong draw to keep the smoke moving through the convoluted passages. Each fire was independent, giving the chance to attend to one without disturbing the other. (Queen Street Mill)*

it off up the chimney. The most common design was the Lancashire boiler, which had two fires feeding two tubes.

Electricity generation

By the 1880s electricity was being generated all over the country – mostly by steam engines. Before the idea of the National Grid, electricity was generated locally and separate companies had their own power station, however modest in size. Most electric trams and railway companies had their own generating stations, all driven by steam engines. The most famous was Lots Road power station, opened in 1902 to power the London Underground, as it converted to electricity. Modified and expanded many times, by 1925 it had 40 boilers and 10 turbine-driven alternators. The steam turbine with its naturally high speeds became the main engine to drive

FIG 3.12: *An early turbine used to drive a generator. The rotor can be seen sitting in the lower half of the case whilst one set of static blades can be seen above. There is another set of static blades already in position in the lower half. When closed, these fit in between the rotor blades.*

FIG 3.13: *A typical twin-cylinder workshop engine in the 5 to 10 hp range which would need the minimum of attention. The relatively large flywheel not only smoothed out the engine's running but helped to absorb changes in the load.*

FIG 3.14: *One rather odd but vital type of steam engine is the steam hammer, where steam raises and drops a very heavy weight. This is used as a massive precision hammer to beat red-hot iron and steel into shape. (Black Country Living Museum)*

the alternators and remains so to the present. Modern atomic power stations only use atomic power to produce heat – this is used to generate steam, which drives the turbines. Nearly all of these turbines condense and re-use the steam: just as the water passes through the boiler to be made into steam, the steam passes through a heat exchanger to be cooled and returned to water. The heat extracted in these exchangers is usually passed into the sea or a large local river but sometimes, to prevent over-warming a river, power stations dissipate the heat in massive cooling towers.

CHAPTER 4

Movable Engines

⊢⋅⊣ ⊠◈⊠ ⊢⋅⊣

Τhis chapter looks at steam engines which either move things, or which can be moved to a spot where they do work. This somewhat vague definition covers probably the most familiar range of engines, many of which can be seen working around the country at steam rallies.

Railways and tramways

Trevithick's first experiments with a steam-driven coach were foiled by poor roads so he immediately turned to tramways instead. At first the tracks were not strong enough but very quickly engineers realized the possibilities and the steam engine reigned supreme until its demise in the 1960s. Today, the term 'steam engine' invariably conjures up the image of a steam railway engine, showing how so many other uses have disappeared from the public gaze over the last century.

In many ways the very first locomotives resembled the beam engine but Stephenson's *Rocket* clearly showed the way ahead and by the end of the 1830s steam locomotives had evolved that we would recognize and understand today. The railway engine was the first use of an engine that had to be self-contained – it had to carry its coal and water and was complete with its own boiler and

cylinders. This need to have everything move along track of a fixed gauge, and the weight that the track could support being limited, meant that one couldn't simply make the engine bigger in order to get more power. Instead these restrictions drove a need to improve the performance, which led to a steady series of developments.

Very early on, the boilers used furnace tubes. As described in Chapter 3, the heat and smoke from the fire was drawn through the water in the boiler via multiple tubes, giving a much better transfer of heat into the water. The lack of a tall chimney to draw the fire was solved by having wind deflectors

FIG 4.1: *A very early locomotive built for the Hetton Colliery in County Durham. Notice the cylinders are partly within the boiler and use a beam to drive the long vertical cranks.*

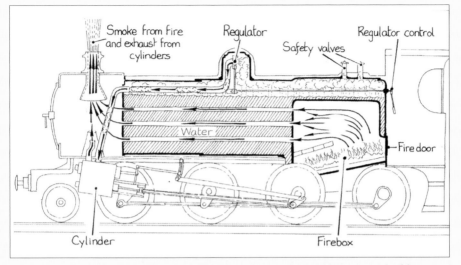

FIG 4.2: *Cross-section of a steam locomotive of the 1850s showing how the blast pipe that sent the spent steam from the cylinders up towards the chimney draws the fire, smoke and fumes through the water in the boiler.*

(dampers) under the fireplace to force air through the burning coal, and most importantly, the spent steam from the cylinders was directed up a short 'blast pipe' placed in line with and below the chimney. By directing a jet of steam up the chimney causes a drop in pressure (the venturi effect) which draws the smoke through the boiler tubes. By the mid 19th century experiments were under way with super-heated steam. This involves taking the steam back through additional pipes within those that carry the fire's heat through the boiler, and thus heating the steam a second time. This raises the temperature still further and increases the amount of energy in the steam. Initially there were no lubricants that could withstand these higher temperatures but these were soon developed and most top-of-the-range locomotives used super-heated steam after the 1880s.

Cylinder layout changed very little from the double-acting horizontal arrangement, though three and four cylinders were tried, as was compound working. The valves were always the difficult part, since they have to work over a wide range of speeds and to provide a fully controllable cut-off facility to allow the driver to vary how long full-pressure steam would be admitted to the cylinders. These engines also had to be able to reverse and run freely in either direction, again solved by clever operation of the valve gear.

FIG 4.3: *A most romantic sight, a steam engine in full flight, photographed in 1951 when steam was still supreme.*

Trams did not begin to ply our streets in any numbers until about 1860, and horse-drawn trams were the norm. The use of steam trams started in Glasgow in 1877 and peaked during the 1890s, being particularly common in the Midlands and north. Though a few attempts had been made to build a steam engine within a tram the normal steam tram was simply an unpowered carriage hauled by a small steam locomotive. As these ran through the streets, all moving parts had to be shielded to prevent accidents. The noise and amount of steam emitted was also restricted, giving rise to a standard design, based on an 0–4–0 wheel layout with condensing apparatus, in all weighing around 7 tons. The

locomotive cost much more than a horse but could haul a greater load and often covered a total of 70 miles or more each day. These larger trams could now have a roof over the upper deck (but did not always have one!), and though this saved passengers from getting wet it was possibly intended rather to protect them from smuts and burning ash from the engine. Steam trams carried around 60 passengers, compared with 40 on the horse-drawn trams and, to allow the heavier loads to tackle the tight curves typical of tramways, they were usually carried on two bogies rather than four fixed wheels.

The arrival of electric trams meant that most steam units were retired

FIG 4.4: *Steam trams in Birmingham (a) and Burnley (b) showing the slightly odd skirted loco hauling a single open-top tram car.*

around the turn of the century but a few bravely battled on in the remote parts of Lancashire. There is a blurred area between the urban tramway (track set completely within the roadway) and the rural tramway which was in effect a railway line that followed alongside minor roads. Steam haulage along these rural lines continued into the 1930s.

Steam traction engines

These were possibly the most versatile machines ever made by man! They were the Swiss Army knife of rural life. Bristling with gadgets they could haul other wagons or loads; cable-winding attachments could pull almost anything; a flywheel pulley could drive machinery via a long belt. Traction engines were extensively used on farms for threshing, sawing timber and crushing stone. Special adaptations allowed a long cable to be wound onto a horizontal drum to give the first mechanical means of ploughing a field.

Always fitted with very wide wheels they could move over fairly rough ground and it was this ability that produced another variation – the steamroller used for laying roads. Once a job was complete it could simply drive off to the next task. Like the railway locomotive, traction engines were restrained by size and weight but still had to carry their fuel and water. The engines themselves were usually single-cylinder or two-cylinder compound designs mounted above the boiler. The steering of these machines was invariably by pivoting the front

FIG 4.5: *A lovingly-restored 1912 Wallis & Stephens single-cylinder 8-hp traction engine which spent much of its life driving threshing machines in Wiltshire. To give an idea of the versatility of these machines, this one was used to pull up large trees in preparation for a new airfield.*

FIG 4.6: *The classic thrashing scene recreated at the Bromyard Steam Fair in Herefordshire. Note the large belt-driving wheel which also acted as a flywheel. Many of these engines had a single cylinder and the flywheel was vital in smoothing the power output.*

FIG 4.7: *A large 16-hp twin-cylinder Fowler engine originally ordered by the Ministry of Munitions in 1918, then converted for cable ploughing in the Second World War and seen here demonstrating at the Shrewsbury Steam Rally. The drum mounted below the boiler can hold 800 yards of cable. Two of these machines work together, pulling the plough to and fro between them.*

wheels or roller on a central bearing with a chain attached to the ends of the axle. This chain was wound around a drum rotated by gearing from the steering wheel, so that as one side wound the chain in, the other side's chain was slackened, which turned the front wheel assembly. The driver had to be very alert as, not only was he driving the vehicle through the streets, but also he had to tend the boiler and fire. Though today usually manned by two people there is precious little room to move around in the driving space.

A variation on the traction engine

FIG 4.8: *The Burrell Road Locomotive 'Dorothy' resplendent at the Bromyard Steam Fair. This has a two-cylinder compound engine and, as the maker's name 'Road Locomotive' suggests, this would have been intended for general haulage and construction work.*

was the portable engine. These were just an engine and boiler mounted on a trailer that could be pulled by a horse or another traction engine. Weighing less, they were ideal for powering machinery such as stone crushers and timber saws, where the engine was needed for some time but didn't justify a permanent engine. Yet another variation was the so-called Donkey

FIG 4.9: *Another beautifully-restored Fowler machine, this time a 1913 road roller that worked in Gloucestershire until 1947. Its working life finally ended in 1970. This has a two-cylinder compound engine and weighs in at 12 tons. Note the front roller is split into two parts to help when turning corners, and has a scraper bar to remove dirt or soft tarmac that might stick to the roller.*

engine where the engine was mounted on a simple sledge which could be dragged along by a horse. These could also be moved around by using their own cable winch. The cable end would be secured to a tree and the engine pulled itself along by winding the cable back onto the drum. These were often employed in forestry working where the low centre of gravity and the

FIG 4.10: *A Fowler Super Lion Crane engine from 1929 that worked for John Thompson Boiler Engineers of Wolverhampton until 1958. It was specially steamed in 1960 to move the 10,000th boiler out of the works en route to Rolls-Royce.*

FIG 4.11: *A portable steam engine made by Ransomes, Sims & Jefferies in 1908 which spent its first 30 years driving hop-kiln fans and then steaming pig swill until 1962. Seen here in a typical working situation driving timber-sawing machinery.*

FIG 4.12: *(Right) Another common portable engine – the fire pump. This pre 1880 machine had long served the city of Chester before being restored in 1996.*

relatively low weight meant that these engines could be dragged almost anywhere.

Steam vehicles

Interestingly, these were one of the very first uses for higher-pressure steam engines (Trevithick's experiments in 1802 – see Chapter 2) but they had to wait for better roads before becoming widespread. The arrival of the railways in part delayed the improvements needed in the road system and it was not until the 1880s that steam-driven

FIG 4.13: *The American Stanley Steamer, a Model 85 made in 1910 with a 30-hp oil-fired engine ...*

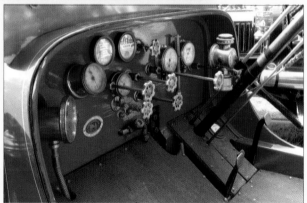

... And just in case you wondered, here's what the driver would see!

FIG 4.14: *An example of the Sentinel steam wagon, this drop-sided version has been put together from three derelict Sentinels and travels to rallies under its own power.*

road vehicles reappear. Though many steam-engined cars were made, the most famous is the American 'Stanley Steamer', which broke record after record for speed, achieving a world record of 127.7 mph in 1906. The earliest models were fired by coal but by the 1890s oil replaced coal, being more efficient and relatively easy to control.

FIG 4.15: *This Foden Steam Bus from 1914 was restored on a flat lorry but shows how a small traction engine could be adapted for different uses.*

Cars at this time were still very much expensive toys and it is in the commercial world that we see the steam engine prosper. By the late 19th century steam wagons (not lorries) were appearing, and these continued to be developed through the early decades of the 20th century. By the 1890s wagons which operated on oil were being produced and, though not that different from a traction engine pulling a cart, the first articulated wagon was produced by the Thornycroft company. Many wagons could be supplied with different bodies: a flat base to carry goods that weren't affected by rain, part-boxed-in wagons using a canvas sheeting, a fully covered body like a modern lorry or open seating to produce a bus. By the first decade of the 20th century almost everything we see today existed – ambulances, Black Marias, richly decorated privately owned wagons, military vehicles, taxis and buses. Company names like Fodens and Leyland (originally the Lancashire Steam Motor Co.) appear in these early years.

There were two basic engine layouts used. The first, called an 'overtype', was similar to a traction engine in that it had a horizontal boiler with the engine above and the driver positioned behind. The other was the 'undertype', where the engine was mounted below the vehicle's chassis. The boiler could

FIG 4.16: *Another Foden product showing just how similar these units were to a traction engine, with the driver's view blocked by the chimney.*

FIG 4.17: *Just a few years later and we have a little protection and pneumatic tyres. It often is not realised that until horse transport ceased the roads were full of nails from the horseshoes – not what the early pneumatic tyres needed!*

be horizontal or vertical and in later versions the driver's position moved in front of the boiler giving a much better view of the road. All the early machines drove the rear axle by means of a chain but some later vehicles used a shaft drive. Despite the arrival of diesel-powered engines, surprisingly little development took place in steam wagons apart from the boiler (as burning diesel requires different arrangements from burning coal). By the 1930s the need to provide a quicker start-up produced quick-heating boilers, ending with the flash boiler where water is turned directly into steam by being dripped onto a suitable hot surface. The diesel lorry was

unstoppable, however, and by 1940 all production of steam vehicles had ended. One interesting use which lingered on into the 1950s was tar laying: since these wagons had heat and hot water as part of their engine it was easy to keep a tank of tar warm and ready to spray on roads. The wagon would be followed by a gritting lorry and then rollers.

Today, work still continues on steam cars, with an attempt at the world speed record planned for 2009 using a propane-fired, turbine-driven car.

Showman's engines

These are a special 20th-century version of the traction engine primarily

FIG 4.18: *A nice example of a road engine built in 1924 by Burrells with a 6-hp compound engine. It was converted to a showman's specification in 1934 but used for threshing during the Second World War and was later found derelict in a hedge in 1965. It is now fully restored to its pre-war glory.*

FIG 4.19: *This example comes from the famous John Fowler Company of Leeds. Showman's engines always have the generator mounted on a characteristic projection over the boiler end, but their road-hauling abilities are just as important. This engine carries very little special decoration and the name 'Plain but Powerful' sums up its road performance. Unfortunately, for the driver, the visibility ahead is almost nil.*

used to move large wagons carrying fairground equipment, but also to generate the electricity used to light the various rides and stalls; always resplendent in beautiful paintwork and shining brass. We forget, with our large, modern articulated lorries, that moving a fair or circus needed many wagons with the showman's engine pulling five or six fully loaded trailers through the towns and countryside.

Boats and ships

Against a background of centuries of sailing ships dependent on the wind and weather, one can imagine the euphoria that greeted the first ship with independent power. This was a paddle steamer, where the engine turned a shaft which extended across the craft, driving a large paddle on each side. This needed a low turning speed and the early beam engine was ideal. One problem was that the engine was heavy: as the paddle shaft had to be above the waterline the first attempts put the beam engine above the shaft giving a very high centre of gravity, and this arrangement was used on large ferries in America. Various approaches evolved to get the engine lower in the boat. The most common was to have

FIG 4.20: *The paddle steamer* Waverly, *showing just how wide the paddle wheels are. Built in 1947 and driven by a triple-cylinder compound engine, she is the last sea-going paddle steamer in the world.*

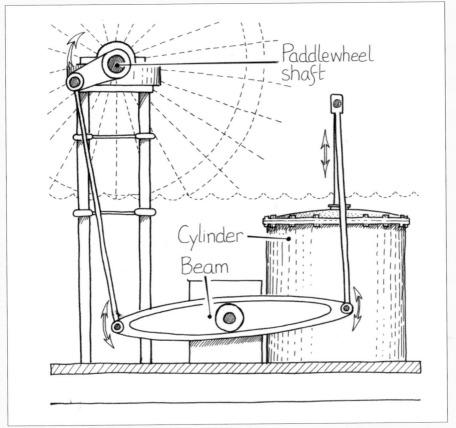

Paddlewheel shaft

Cylinder

Beam

FIG 4.21: *A simplified drawing showing how the early beam engine was adapted for use in paddle steamers. This placed the weight below the paddle wheel shaft, keeping the ship's centre of gravity low and the ship stable in the water.*

the beam mounted at the base of the engine driving a paddle shaft mounted above the engine. Though paddle steamers gave way to propeller-driven ships, they continued to be produced into the 20th century as they could be built to move on very shallow waters.

The need to carry coal limited the range in steam ships. Early steam ships carried sails which would be used whenever the wind was favourable to save coal. Brunel was one of the first to realize that, with greater ship size, the storage capacity of ships increased far more than the energy needed to push them through the water and so he solved the distance problem – build big! The engines themselves developed with

FIG 4.22: *A preserved paddle-steamer engine, one of a pair that worked side by side, giving superb control over the ship.*

FIG 4.23: *For many years steam engines were used on working narrowboats on the English canal system. The most famous of the preserved ones is* President, *seen here at Braunston.*

FIG 4.24: *A three-cylinder compound engine of the type that would have been used in ships before the turbine burst so rudely onto the scene. Along the top are the three cylinders, each larger in diameter than the previous one. Between the cylinders and the flywheels can be seen the two inter-cylinder reservoirs which enabled the three cylinders to operate 120 degrees apart giving a very smooth delivery of power to the crankshaft. This is one of the many engines on display in the Kew Bridge Steam Museum.*

time, including the use of compound engines and condensing the steam exhaust to recover the water. I can remember crossing to the Isle of Wight in the 1950s on paddle steamers that used a beautiful horizontal steam engine to turn the paddles. Once the propeller had proved successful most new ships used multi-cylinder compound engines mounted, like the propeller shaft, low down inside the ship.

CHAPTER 5

The Scene Today

T oday we must thank the bands of enthusiasts who prevented old steam engines from being scrapped, aided at times by water companies who at least could see the need to preserve these wonderful machines for new generations to enjoy. I doubt, though, if any realized that we would have many massive beam engines working once again under steam plus many stationary engines chugging away in museums. The preservation of steam railways is probably better known but no less remarkable. To complete the picture we have rallies around the country to which traction engines, stationary engines and showman's engines come to entertain and delight the visitors.

I have listed here some of the museums that have steam engines on display, many having 'in steam' days, plus some of the major preserved steam-railway sites. For information on steam rallies one can do no better than refer to *Old Glory* magazine, usually stocked by WH Smith and other large newsagents.

FIG 5.1: *A medley of steam engines prepare for the traditional tour around the show ground at the Shrewsbury Steam Rally.*

General museums that have steam engines in addition to many other industrial heritage exhibits

Black Country Living Museum, Dudley. 0121 5579643
www.bclm.co.uk
British Engineerium, Hove. 01273 554070
www.britishengineerium.com
Cambridge Museum of Technology. 01223 368650
www.museumoftechnology.com
Discovery Museum, Newcastle. 0191 2326789
www.twmuseums.org.uk
Iron Bridge Museum – Blists Hill, Telford. 01952 433522
www.ironbridge.org.uk
Museum of Science and Industry, Manchester. 0161 8321380
www.msim.org.uk
Science Museum, London. 020 7942 4000
www.nmsi.ac.uk
Think Tank, Birmingham. 0121 3031655
www.thinktank.ac

Most of the sites listed below are staffed by volunteers and are not open or in steam on a daily basis. Many have websites and these should be checked for opening details; or phone before setting out on a long journey.

Abbey Pumping Station, Leicester. 0116 2995111
www.leicester.gov.uk/your-council—services/lc/leicester-city-museums/museums/abbey-pumping-station
Broomy Hill Waterworks Museum, Hereford. 01432 344062
www.waterworksmuseum.org.uk
Caudwell's Mill, Rowsley, Derbyshire. 01629 734374
www.cressbrook.co.uk/visits/caudwell.php
Claymills Pumping Station, Streeton, Burton on Trent. 01283 509929
www.claymills.org.uk
Coleham Pumping Station, Shrewsbury. 01743 362947
www.shrewsburymuseums.com/coleham
Cornish Mines & Engines, Pool. 01209 315027
www.chycor.co.uk/tourism/cata-guest/cornish-mines/cornish-mines.htm
Crofton Pumping Station, Nr Swindon. 01672 870300
www.katrust.org
Eastney Beam Engine, Portsmouth. 02392 827261
www.memorials.inportsmouth.co.uk/southsea/beam-engine-house.htm

Ellenroad Engine House, Milnrow.   01706 8481952
www.ellenroad.org.uk
Elsecar Heritage Centre, Barnsley. 01226 740203
www.elsecar-heritage-centre.co.uk
Garlogie Mill Power House, Nr Aberdeen.   01771 622906
Hollycombe Steam Collection, Liphook.   01428 724900
www.hollycombe.co.uk
Industrial Steam Museum, Forncett St Mary, Nr Norwich.   01508 488277
www.oldenginehouse.demon.co.uk
Kew Bridge Steam Museum, Brentford.   020 8568 4757
www.kbsm.org
Long Shop Steam Museum, Leiston.   01728 832189
www.longshop.care4free.net
Markham Grange Steam Museum, Brodsworth, Nr Doncaster.   01302 330430
www.mgsteam.btinternet.co.uk

A long-lost sight, a steam-driven fairground ride. Fortunately several of these machines have been preserved. This engine bears the delightful name of Lady Go Lightly.

Papplewick Pumping Station, Ravenshead.   0115 9632938
www.papplewickpumpingstation.co.uk
Pinchbeck Marsh Engine & Land Drainage Museum, Nr Boston.   01775 725468
Queen Street Mill, Harle Syke, Burnley.   01282 412555
www.lancashire.gov.uk/acs/sites/museums/venues/qsm/
Ryhope Pumping Station, Sunderland.   0191 5210235
www.g3wte.demon.co.uk
Shore Rd Pumping Station, Birkenhead.   0151 6501182
www.wirral.gov.uk/LGCL/100009/200070/1017/content_0000525.html
Strumpshaw Old Hall Steam Engine Museum, Nr Gt Yarmouth.   01603 713392
www.strumpshawsteammuseum.co.uk
Top Engine House, Middleton by Winksworth.   01629 823204
Westonzoyland Pumping Station, Nr Bridgwater.   01823 275795
www. wzlet.org

Steam Railway Sites

There are a great number of sites which feature steam locomotives, some small, some very large. Below is a short selection of my favourites, all of which carry passengers.

Bluebell Railway, Sheffield Park, E. Sussex.   01825 720800
www.bluebell-railway.co.uk
Bodmin & Wenford Railway, Bodmin.   01208 73666
www.bodminandwenfordrailway.co.uk
Churnet Valley Railway, Cheddleton, Nr Leek.   08707 666312
www.churnet-valley-railway.co.uk
Dean Forest Railway, Norchard, Lydney.   01594 845840
www.deanforestrailway.co.uk
Gloucester Warwickshire Railway, Toddington.   01242 621405
www.gwsr.com
Great Central Railway, Loughborough.   01509 230726
www.gcrailway.co.uk
Isle of Wight Steam Railway, Havenstreet.   01983 882204
www.iwsteamrailway.co.uk
Keighley & Worth Valley Railway, Keighley.   01535 645214
www.kwvr.co.uk
Kent & East Sussex Railway, Tenterden.   01580 765155
www.kesr.org.uk
Llangollen Railway, Llangollen.   01978 860979
www.llangollen-railway.co.uk
Mid-Hants Railway, Alresford.   01962 733810
www.watercressline.co.uk

Nene Valley Railway, Peterborough.   01780 784444
www.nvr.org.uk
North Norfolk Railway, Sheringham.   01263 820800
www.nnr.co.uk
North Yorkshire Moors Railway, Pickering.   01751 472508
www.northyorkshiremoorsrailway.com
Paignton & Dartmouth Steam Railway, Devon.   01803 555872
www.paignton-steamrailway.co.uk
Severn Valley Railway, Bewdley.   01299 403816
www.svr.co.uk
South Devon Railway, Buckfastleigh.   01364 642338
www.southdevonrailway.org
Swanage Railway, Swanage.   01929 425800
www.swanagerailway.co.uk
West Somerset Railway, Minehead.   01643 704996
www.west-somerset-railway.co.uk

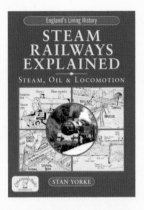

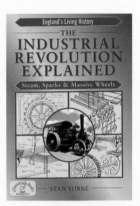

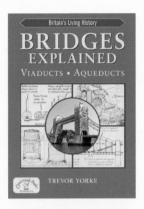

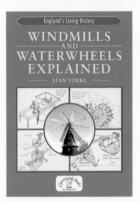

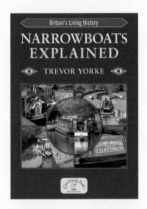

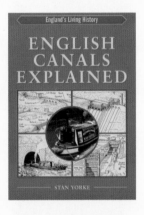

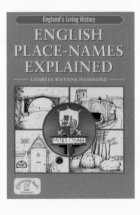

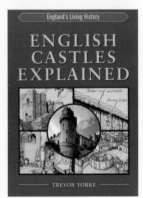

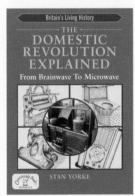